Plantation Row
Slave Cabin Cooking

The Roots of Soul Food

Patricia B. Mitchell

Published 1998 by the author at the
Sims-Mitchell House Bed & Breakfast,
P. O. Box 429, Chatham, VA 24531.
    Tel/fax: 804-432-0595
    E-mail: answers@foodhistory.com
    Website: www.foodhistory.com

Printed in the U. S. A.
ISBN 0-925117-89-7

Sixth Printing, May 2001

- *Illustrations* -

Front cover - *Detail adapted from illustration "Southern
Scenes — Cooking Shrimps," Frank Leslie's, 1877.*

Inside title page - *Detail from illustration, "Feeding
Negro Children at Hilton Head, South Carolina,"
Harper's Pictorial History of the Great Rebellion
in the United States, 1866.*

Back cover - *Drawing after illustration on container label
designed by Walls & Co., Ltd., New Orleans, LA,
for "Cake Walk Brand Oysters," Barataria Canning
Company, Biloxi, MS, ca. 1900.*

Table of Contents

To Begin

From cabin to condominium, and from plantation kitchen to today's stylish restaurants, black cooking has satisfied and sustained bodies and souls. In fact, as chef Louis P. DeGouy noted in 1947, "No statement of the excellence of the cooking of American homemakers, who are representative of every race of mankind, is complete without a reference to the fine cooking of the Negroes of the South, who are natural gourmets." [1]

In this book, we will contemplate the history and foodways which are the roots of soul food.

A Look at Numbers

In the mid-1600's there were slightly more slaves in the Northern colonies than in the Southern, and in both regions the total number was under a thousand. In the mid-1700's, approximately 50,000 blacks were enslaved in the North, and about 500,000 in the South. By 1860, almost all slaves lived in the South. Their numbers reached four million. [2]

However, only about one-fourth of whites in the South had slaves or were members of slave-owning families. The average white citizens did their own work. Among slaveholders, fewer than 1 percent of the laborlords owned 100 or more slaves. In fact, in 1850 over half the slaveholders possessed fewer than five slaves. The concept of a white-columned mansion located on thousands of verdant acres owned by one Caucasian and served by thousands of dark-skinned people is mythical. It is said that in the heyday of the slavery system, fewer than half a dozen slaveowners held as many as a thousand slaves. [3]

Nevertheless, slave labor was very important to the plantation economy. On big non-mechanized plantations where cotton, sugar cane, rice, or tobacco were grown, many hands were necessary. "My master owned over a hundred grown slaves and the children were thick as blackbirds," Melvin Smith recollected. "Some worked in the master's house, some did the washing, others drove the horses and others did the same kind of work for the overseer." [4]

Long Hours

Field hands generally worked Monday through Saturday noon, getting the rest of Saturday and Sundays off. A wake-up call was sounded at 4 a.m. when a bugle, conchshell, or a ram's horn was blown. James Bolton remembered, "My master didn't have no bell. He had them blow bugles for to wake up his hands and to call them from the fields. . . . Mistress done learned the cook to count the clock. None of the rest of [us] could count the clock." [5]

Callie Elder recalled, "[T]he men had to be in the fields by sunrise. The womans went out about eight o'clock. They stopped work at sundown and by the time they ate and done the chores for the day it was ten o'clock before they hit the bed." [6]

"We worked from see to can't," commented Willis Winn. [7] Slaves could also be hired out to other individuals or enterprises. For example, in May and June, 1829, contractors advertised in the *Virginia Herald* for laborers, preferably black, to work on the construction of the Rappahannock River Canal. They needed 50 to 60 able-bodied men, and promised $5 - $7 a month, plus "as much bread, meat, fish and molasses as can be consumed three times a day, with some spirits." The cash went to the slaveholder, although some owners allowed the slave to keep a portion of the hire money as a work incentive. [8]

During their "free time" on weekends slaves might cultivate their garden plots, make repairs on their cabins, wash and mend clothes, or tend to other chores. They often socialized and organized dance sessions called frolics. (Slaves were sometimes even permitted to leave the plantation property to visit neighboring slave quarters.) Christmas, Easter, New Year's, and the Fourth of July might also provide a day of respite for the slaves, although some house servants had to continue their daily ministrations.

Dance Away the Blues

When slaves had an opportunity to dance, ingenious instruments were played. Fiddles made out of gourds with horsehair strings could ring out a melody,[9] or someone might blow a flute-like sound on "quills." (Quills were whistles made out of long reeds or bark which had been perforated. Several could be connected, each with a different tone.[10])

John Cole declared, "Stretch cow-hides over cheese-boxes and you had tambourines. Saw bones from off a cow, knock them together and call it a drum. Or use broom-straws on fiddle-strings, and you had your entire band." [11]

Tin buckets and pans could also be beaten as drums. Sometimes in good weather dancers carried blazing torches of kindling wood for light, or danced around a fire.[12] (In bad weather the interior of a slave's cabin was used for the gathering.) Dances especially enjoyed were the juba (from the African "giouba"[13]), the pigeon wing, Buzzard Lope, Mary Jane, and Turkey Trot. According to Estella Jones:

"Cake walking was a lot of fun during slavery time. They swept the yards real clean and set benches around for the party. Banjoes was used for music making. The womens wore long, ruffled dresses with hoops in them and the mens had on high hats, long split-tailed coats, and some of them used walking sticks. The couple that danced best got a prize. Sometimes the slave owners come to these parties because they enjoyed watching the dance, and they decided who dance the best. Most parties during slavery time, was give on Saturday night during work seasons, but during winter they was give on most any night." [14]

Annie Wallace recounted the following:

"You know they used to wear petticoats starched with hominy water. They were starched so stiff that every time you stopped they would pop real loud. Well, [Mother] would go out at night to a party some of the colored folks was havin' and she would tell us kids to stay in the house and open the door in a hurry when we heard her acomin'. And when we heared them petticoats apoppin' as she run down the path, we'd open the door wide and she would get away from the patteroll [patroller]." [16]

Fannie Berry gave a detailed dance description:

"Used to go over to de Saunders place fo' dancin'. Musta been hundred slaves over thar, an' they always had de bes' dances. Mos' times fo' de dance dey had Dennis to play de banjer. Dennis had a twisted arm, an' he couldn't do much work, but he sho' could pick dat banjer. Gals would put on dey spare dress ef dey had one, an' men would put a clean shirt on. Gals always tried to fix up fo' partyin', even ef dey ain't got nothin' but a piece of ribbon to tie in dey hair. Mos' times wear yo' shoes to de dance an' den take 'em off. Dem ole hard shoes make too much noise, an' hurt yo' feet. Couldn't do no steppin' in dem field shoes.

"Wasn't none of this sinful dancin' where yo' partner off wid man an woman squeezed up close to one another. Danced 'spectable, de slaves did, shiftin' 'round fum one partner to 'nother an' holdin' one 'nother out at arm's length.

"What kind of dances? Well, dey wasn't no special name to 'em. Dere was cuttin' de pigeons wings — dat was flippin' yo' arms an' legs roun' an' holdin' yo' neck stiff like a bird do. Den dere was gwine to de east, an' gwine to de west — dat was wid partners an' sometimes dey got to kiss each other, but dey stan' back an' kiss widout wrappin' no arms roun' like de young folks do today. An' dere was callin' de figgers an' dat meant dat de fiddler would call de number an' all de couples got to cut dat number.

"Set de flo'? Dat was — well de couples would do dat in turn. Dey come up an' bend over toward each other at de waist, an' de woman put her hands on her hips an' de man roll his eyes all roun' an' grin an' dey pat do flo' wid dey feet jus' like dey was puttin' it in place. Used to do dat bes' on dirt flo' so de feet could slap down hard against it. Sometimes dey would set de flo' alone — either a man or a woman. Den dey would set a glass of water on dey haid an' see how many kinds of steps dey could make widout spillin' de water.

*"Dancin' on de spot was de same thing as set de
flo' — almos'. Jus' mean you got to stay in de circle.
De fiddler would take a charred corn-cob an' draw a
circle on de flo', den call one arter de odder up an'
dance in de circle. Effen yo' feet tetch de edge you is
out. Dat was jus' like a cake-walk, 'cause sometime
dey bake a cake an' give it to de one dat did de mos'
steps on de spot. No, I never did win no cake, but I
was purty good at it jus' de same, I reckon.* " [16]

Bailey Cunningham added more:

*"We did the 'buck dance.' A boy and girl would
hold hands and jump up and down and swing around
keeping time with the music. We would dance awhile
then go to the other room and drink coffee, corn whisky
or apple brandy . . . . We would dance and play all
night but had to be ready to work next day.* " [17]

Work Parties

Authorized quilting parties provided an opportunity for
slaves to gather in a cabin and work on bed quilts for their
use. The quilts were usually "pieced up" by the elderly slaves
who were no longer able to work in the fields. Scraps of old
material from garments, ticking, grain sacks, whatever, were
cut out, and perhaps dyed, for the quilts. Sometimes new
gingham or calico cloth was used. Cotton or wool batting or
other filling or interlining was layered between the backing
and the patterned top of the quilt. Red was a favorite color.
Patterns such as the Star of Bethlehem, the fish tail, and the
swan's nest were popular, as well as the random patchwork
"crazy quilt" design. [18]

At the winter evening "quilting bees" men even
participated. Four people usually worked on sewing together
a quilt, one person at each corner. On some plantations a
prize was given to the four who finished their quilt first. [19]

As busy fingers and needles flew, tongues flew, too.
Quilting parties provided an excellent opportunity for
conversation and storytelling. Current gossip, discussion of
events and ideas, and personal recollections kept minds and

mouths busy. Creative storytellers had a captive audience if they wished to "spin a yarn."

After the evening's work was done, refreshments were served, and musical instruments taken up to provide dance music. Some masters provided whiskey for the gatherings. Other labor parties included corn huskings, cotton pickings, pea shellings, "completion of crop planting" parties, and feasts at hog-killing time. Masters or overseers frequently appointed a "general" to lead quick tempo work songs to speed the pace of labor, and often offered a reward to the person who accomplished the most.

"Corn shuckin's was the thing them days," Willis Winn recalled. "I liked to see them come. They cooked up guineas and ducks and chickens and sometimes roast a pig."[20]

John Finnely, age 86, reminisced:

"We had some joyments on de plantation, no parties or dancin' but we had de corn huskin' and de [black] fights. For de corn huskin' everybody come to one place and dey gives de prize for findin' de red ear. On Massa's place de prize am brandy or you am allowed to kiss de gal you calls for. While us huskin' us sing lots, but, I'se not gwine sing any dem songs, 'cause I'se forget and my voice sound like de bray of de mule."[21]

Spritual Enrichment

Slaves usually attended their white owner's church, although they walked while he and his family rode. James Bolton recalled walking nine miles to church.[22] Shoes were scarce and uncomfortable. Another former slave said, "Grandma put her shoes in her pockets and when we got within a mile of the church she put her shoes on . . . ."[23]

The slaves had to sit in the back of the building, sometimes behind a partition; or in a gallery, which often had a separate outside door and staircase leading up to it. First the white pastor gave a sermon to the Caucasians, then he addressed the blacks.

Cornelius Garner commented:

"De preaching us got 'twon't nothing much. Dat ole white preacher just was telling us slaves to be good to our marsters. We ain't keer'd a bit 'bout dat stuff he was telling us 'cause we wanted to sing, pray, and serve God in our own way. You see, 'legion needs a little motion — specially if you gwine feel de spirret." [24]

"Ole white preachers used to talk wid dey tongues widdout sayin' nothin' but Jesus told us slaves to talk wid our hearts," Nancy Williams explained. She added, in telling how she accepted salvation, "[I] Feared I miss de substince an' ketch de shadow." However, after six months of soul-searching the Spirit "struck her." [25]

Sometimes slaves were permitted to listen to black men who had convinced the master that God had called them to preach. These "cheerbackers" were allowed to preach in and around the slave quarters after work hours. [26] In some instances white ministers came on a regular basis to preach to the slaves in their quarters. [27]

Charlie Hudson gave this account:

"There warn't no church for slaves where us was. Marse David give us a pass so us wouldn't be disturbed [by patrollers] and let us go around from one plantation to another on Sundays for prayer meetings in the cabins and under trees if the weather was warm and nice." [28]

Clara Young shared this memory:

"De most fun we had was at our [church] meetin's. We had them most every Sunday and dey lasted way into de night. De preacher I liked de best . . . sure could read out of his hand. He never learned no real readin' and writin' but he sure knowed his Bible and would hold his hand out and make like he was readin' and preach de purtiest preachin' you ever heard. De meetin's last from early in de mornin' till late at night. When dark come, de men folks would

hang up a wash pot, bottom upwards, in de little brush church house us had, so's it would catch de noise and de overseer wouldn't hear us singin' and shoutin'. Dey didn't mind us meetin' in de daytime, but dey thought iffen we stayed up half de night we wouldn't work so hard de next day — and dat was de truth." [29]

The use of pots or tubs to keep sound from traveling seems to be related to West African religious practices. [30]

Campmeetings, revivals, baptisms, and dinner on the grounds were church activities fondly described by ex-slaves. Willis Cofer gave this account:

"The sure enough big days was them camp meeting days. White folks and [blacks] all went to the same camp meeting, and they brung plenty along to eat — big old loafs of light bread what had been baked in the skillets. The night before they sat it in the ovens to rise and by morning it had done rise to the top of the deep old pans. They piled the red coals all around the ovens and when that bread got done it was good enough for anybody. The tables was loaded with barbecued pigs and lambs and all the fried chicken folks could eat, and all sorts of pies and cakes was spread out with the other goodies." [31]

Dressed for Work

The regular clothing of slaves was utilitarian. Slaves living in cities, rather than on the large, self-sustaining plantations, dressed in garments made of "Negro cloth." Manufactured in northern or English factories, the term referred to material made from left-over thread. This could include calicos, duck, kerseys, linsey-woolsey, jeans, nankeens, and tows. The cloth was generally made into clothing of two sizes — small or large. [32]

On some big plantations, looms and seamstresses were kept busy producing clothes for the black workers. Well-provisioned slaves typically had one change of clothing.

Women wore dresses with low waists and gathered skirts. Men wore britches and coarse, simply-styled work shirts. Often natural dyes were used to color the cloth. "They used indigo for blue, oak bark for brown, green husks often for black, and sumacs for red, and they'd mix these colors to make other colors," recalled James Bolton. [33]

Children of both sexes wore sack-shaped shirts. Sometimes the boys became embarrassingly mature for such garments before they were "graduated" to long britches.

Booker Taliaferro Washington, the famous educator, wrote about his early wardrobe:

"One thing I remember more vividly than any other in connection with the days when I was a slave was my dress, or, rather, my lack of dress.

"The years that the war was in progress between the States were especially trying to the slaves, so far as clothing were concerned. The Southern white people found it extremely hard to get clothing for themselves during that war, and, of course, the slaves underwent no little suffering in this respect. The only garment that I remember receiving from my owners during the war was a 'tow shirt.' When I did not wear this shirt I was positively without any garment. This shirt was made of the refuse flax that grew in that part of Virginia, and it was a veritable instrument of torture. It was stiff and coarse. Until it had been worn for about six weeks it made one feel as if a thousand needle points were pricking his flesh. I suppose I was about six years old when I was given one of these shirts to wear. After repeated trials the torture was more than my childish flesh could endure and I gave it up in despair. To this day the sight of a new shirt revives the recollection of the torture of my first new shirt. In the midst of my despair, in connection with this garment, my brother John, who was about two years older than I, did me a kindness which I shall never forget. He volunteered to wear my new shirt for me until it was 'broken in.' After he had worn it for several weeks I ventured to wear it myself, but not without pain." [34]

Black children usually went barefoot. "Our foots cracked open 'till they looked like goose foots," [35] declared Callie Elder. The brass-toed brogans and the stiff wrap-around shoes worn by adults were often ill-fitting whether made by the plantation cobbler or "store-bought." John Eubanks, a slave in Kentucky, noted that blacks on his plantation "didden have much clothes" and "no shoes." "Come de wintah," he reported, "it be so cold mah feet weah plumb numb mos' o' de time and many a time — when we git a chanct — we druve the hogs . . . from outen the bogs an' put ouah feet in the wahmed wet mud . . . ." [36]

One slave put it: "We prays for the end of tribulations and the end of beatings and for shoes that fit our feet." [37]

Zoned Housing

Many plantations were all-inclusive. The complex might include the Big House, a guest cottage, the overseer's house, slave quarters, a "sick house" or infirmary, a graveyard, kitchen, root cellar, barn, stables, carriage house, blacksmith shop, smokehouse, ice house, and corncrib. Chicken coops and duck houses were common. Some plantations had a loom house and a grist — or other type of — mill; some had "lying-in" houses where nursing mothers stayed. Occasionally a chapel, schoolhouse, slave jail, or whiskey still could be found on the property.

George Washington Browning spoke of a tannery operated by his Uncle Ben on the plantation where they lived. His Uncle Nelson ground the corn at the mill, and also did carpentry work. Uncle Joe was a waggoner and cared for the livestock on the estate. Uncle Bob was the blacksmith. His father Cicero was the shoe maker. "It was not necessary for master to have to buy anything for himself or his families," Browning pointed out. [38]

The cabins in which slaves lived were called slave quarters. The slaves' homes were not fine houses, although some were as good or better than the dwellings of frontier or working-class white people. The appearance of the cabins varied — some were made of logs daubed with mud; some were plank construction; there were even brick slave cabins.

The overseer or slave foreman might live in a slightly nicer home with better furnishings, located in a more desirable spot (such as on a rise in the ground above the other cabins). The cabins of the house servants were built close to the plantation house. The cook often lived over the kitchen. The cabins had one to three rooms, and most housed one family. A fireplace provided heat, and was also used for cooking.

The following is part of a description of Magnolia Plantation near Woodville, Mississippi. It was written by David Holt, a white Mississippian, at the time of the Civil War. .

"The negroes lived in comfortable frame houses built on both sides of a broad street. Each house had a vegetable garden and a chicken yard and the slaves were encouraged to supplement the rations they drew with what they raised. The white overseer lived in a commodious house at one end of the street, and the black 'driver' lived at the other end. This whole place, called 'the quarters,' was surrounded by a fence. 'De white folks up to de house' would buy at the market price, and for cash every egg and chicken that the negroes cared to sell. The chief vegetable raised in the quarters was collards. The lower leaves were eaten for greens. Every slave family was permitted to keep a cow if they would agree to raise the calf; however, many cows were milked on the plantation and the milk distributed among the negroes.

"The weekly rations for an adult negro was four pounds of salt pork, a peck of corn meal, a pint of molasses, some salt, soda and home-made soap. When fresh meat was killed, an extra ration of meat was given to them. The slaves drew rations every Saturday according to their family needs. Wesley, another valuable slave, handed out the rations." [39]

On the Inside, Looking Out

Not all quarters sound as pleasant as those at Magnolia Plantation.

The few windows found in slave cabins usually did not have glass panes. Rough plank shutters were common. One former slave, Robert Shepherd, recalled, "For a window, they just cut a opening in a log and fixed a piece of plank across it so it would slide when they wanted to open or close it." [40]

Booker T. Washington described the home of his birth:

"As nearly as I can get at the facts, I was born in the year 1858 or 1859. At the time I came into the world no careful registry of births of people of my complexion was kept. My birth place was near Hale's Ford, in Franklin County, Virginia. . . . I remember very distinctly the appearance of the cabin in which I was born and lived until freedom came. It was a small log cabin about 12 x 16 feet, and without windows. There was no floor, except a dirt one. There was a large opening in the center of the floor, where sweet potatoes were kept for my master's family during the winter. In this cabin my mother did the cooking, the greater part of the time, for my master's family. Our bed, or 'pallet,' as we called it, was made every night on the dirt floor. Our bed clothing consisted of a few rags gathered here and there." [41]

The slave cabins were sparsely furnished. Some occupants had little more than a bench, a table, and places to sleep. Many slaves slept on the dirt floor on pallets. Other slaves slept in beds constructed with a wooden frame. In 1938, Jasper Battle, a former slave, described the beds: "[The] best of them was corded. They made holes in the sides and foots and headpieces, and run heavy home-made cords in them holes. They wove them crossways in and out of them holes from one side to another 'till they had them ready to lay the mattress mat on." [42]

The mattress was homespun material, usually cotton, stuffed with grass; hay; or wheat, rye, or oat straw. [43] Charlie Hudson, once a slave in Georgia, remarked that the wheat straw used in mattresses was called "Georgy feathers." [44]

Aaron Jones of Marshall County, Mississippi, spoke of "ticks stuffed with shucks and rye. . . . They was pretty comfortable." [45]

-12-

Neal Upson recalled, "[We] never seen no iron springs them days. Them cords, criss-crossed from one side of the bed to the other, was our springs . . . If us didn't tighten them every few days them beds was apt to fall down with us."[46]

To remind people of the advisability of taut ropes so that the bed would not sag uncomfortably or collapse, the expression "sleep tight" came into use.[47]

Most slaves lacked pillows, but if a person was privileged enough to have such, it probably was cotton or "was stuffed with hay what had a little cotton mixed in it sometimes."[48] South Carolinian Peter Clifton proudly recalled, " . . . dat Mammy had a chicken feather pillow she made from de feathers she saved at de kitchen."[49]

Occasionally slaves did receive cast-off furniture and clothes from the master's house. They were provided a few rudimentary utensils for cooking in the cabin fireplaces. (Most slaves were expected to prepare the evening meal, and possibly breakfast, in their individual quarters; during work hours, the plantation cook prepared communal food.)

Home Is Where the Hearth Is

Rhodus Walton remembered "The [cooking] equipment consisted of a iron pot suspended by a hanger and a skillet with long legs that enabled the cook to place fire beneath it."[50]

Benny Dillard reminisced,

"The fireplaces was a heap bigger than they has now, for all the cooking was done in open fireplaces then. 'Taters and cornpone was roasted in the ashes and most of the other victuals was boiled in the big old pots what swung on cranes over the coals. They had long-handled frying pans and heavy iron skillets with big, thick, tight-fitting lids and ovens of all sizes to bake in. All of them things was used right there in the fireplace. There never was no better tasting something to eat than that cooked in them old cook-things in open fireplaces."[51]

"Mighty Good Eatments"

During slavery times, those in bondage were not often given freedom to express themselves in the graphic arts, literature, or fashion. Slave artisans had some opportunity to exercise their skill and creativity in carpentry, masonry, and similar practical work, but it was the black cook, when she cooked for her white owners, who had the raw materials and time to be supremely creative. Even when cooking in their cabins, slaves had a chance to be innovative in utilizing their rationed ingredients and foods foraged from forest, field, and stream. So it was, that when slaves ate or made music, they were best able to express themselves, to reveal their souls. (Some slaves could dress according to their tastes for Saturday night entertainments and for church, if they had the opportunity to buy fashion accessories, jewelry, and the like. This money could be earned through the sale of quilts, eggs, etc.)

After the Emancipation, many impoverished white families of the post-Civil War South turned to blacks for instruction in coaxing crops from poor soil, and turning previously-disdained foodstuffs into satisfying eatables. (The less privileged white yeoman farmers had been growing and eating "humble" foods all along.)

The black cook, like her West African ancestors, used six basic cooking techniques: boiling in water; steaming in leaves; roasting in the fire; baking in ashes; toasting beside the fire; and frying in deep oil.

The Afro-American cook had certain culinary tendencies: the abundant use of leafy green vegetables; the utilization of okra, or nuts and seeds, as thickeners; the addition of peppery/spicy hot sauces; the use of smoked meat for flavoring; the preparation of various kinds of fritters; and the creation of many one-pot dishes composed primarily of rice with "enhancements." [62]

The following accounts document some of the aforementioned techniques and tendencies:

"Us had everything good to eat. Marse Thomas was a rich man and fed [us] . . . well. They cooked in a big open fire place and boiled greens and some of the other victuals in a great big pot what swung on a rack.

Meat, fish and chickens was fried in a griddle iron what was set on a flat-topped trivet with slits to let the fire through. Hoe cakes made of cornmeal and wheat flour sure was good cooked on that griddle. 'Taters was roasted in the ashes, and they cooked bread what they called ash cake in the coals. " [53]

"Mammy used ter bake ash-cakes; dey wuz made wid meal, wid a little salt and mixed wid water; den mammy would rake up de ashes in de fire-place, den she would make up de meal in round cakes, and put dem on de hot bricks ter bake; wen dey hed cooked roun' de edges, she would put ashes on de top ob dem, and wen dey wuz nice and brown, she took dem out and washed dem off wid water. " [54]

"When we roasted a chicken, we got it all nice and clean, stuffed him with dressing, greased him all over good, put a cabbage leaf on the floor of the fireplace, put the chicken on the cabbage leaf, then covered him good with another cabbage leaf, and put hot coals over and around him, and left him to roast. That is the best way to cook chicken. " [55]

"[We] would cook in ashes. We could get old cabbage leaves and wrap up corn pones in it, and rake the ashes and put them in hot ashes to cook. We would wrap potatoes up in cabbage leaves, too, and cook them in ashes. " [56]

"Everybody cooked on open fireplaces them days. They had swinging racks what they called cranes to hang the pots on for boiling. There was ovens for baking and the heavy iron skillets had long handles. One of them old skillets was so big that Mammy could cook thirty biscuits in it at one time. " [57]

"We et yellow bread and greens and black-eyed peas and pot likker and sopped 'lasses. Us and the white folks all cooked in fireplaces. A big iron pot hung out in the yard for to boil greens and hog jowl and such like. We didn't know nothin' about bakin'

powder and made our soda from burnt cobs. That's just as good soda as this Arm and Hammer you get in the store [now]. " [58]

"Next thing I knowed, here come my mistis, and . she say: 'Now Cheney, I want some pone bread for dinner.' Dem hickory coals in dat fireplace was all time ready and hot. They wouldn't be no finger prints left on dat pone when Cheney got through pattin' it out, neither. Better not! Look like dem chillen just couldn't get 'nough of dat hard corn bread. Plenty of fancy coogin' [cooking] went on round dat fireplace, but somehow de pot licker and pone bread 'longside with de fresh buttermilk stirs my memory [more] than anything. " [59]

Aron Carter of Lincoln County, Mississippi, looked back in time:

"De eats wuz good; better dan ah' gets now by a long shot. Dere wuz greens, bacon, peas, rice, milk, butter, loads of fish, possum, rabbits, birds — jes' eberythin'. " [60]

"We don't have nothin' to eat now like we did then. All kinds of game, wild ducks, geese, squirrels, rabbits, possum, pigeons, and fried chicken. My, women in those days could cook! Great big pound cakes a foot and a half high. You don't see such things, nowadays. " [61]

(The slave narratives were collected in the late 1930's, a time of faltering U.S. economy.)

"Sawsidge" Country Style

In plantation days slaves were routinely issued inferior pig parts, but at butchering time or on special occasions and holidays, they might have received better cuts of meat.[62] The "Big House" cook, of course, worked with choice cuts of pork in preparing the white people's food.

Country or bulk sausage was a welcome breakfast food. Annie Hale, who grew up in a family of nine children, recalled breakfasts of pancakes made with cornmeal or buckwheat, and liver pudding or fried sausage meat. She described homemade sausage "with sage, black and red pepper, salt . . . . They [the rolls of sausage] were kept by wrapping the sausage in corn husks, packing them in cheesecloth bags, and hanging them. They'd get a little moldy but they never spoiled." [63]

* * *

2 lbs. lean pork (such as tenderloin), ground
1 1/2 lbs. backbone fat, ground
2 1/2 tsp. salt
1 1/2 tsp. dried sage [or thyme]
3/4 tsp. black pepper
1/2 tsp. ground red pepper [cayenne]

Combine all ingredients. Shape into two rolls about the size of a rolling pin, flattening the ends. Wrap in plastic wrap, and then aluminum foil. Refrigerate or freeze. When ready to use, unwrap and slice into 1/2-inch patties, and fry. (Some people make individual patties to start with, and freeze them separately.)[64]

Note: In the original recipe, the whole cuts of meat were put through a food chopper. Another thought: You may prefer to use only 1 1/2 tsp. salt and also less cayenne pepper.

Country-Style Salt Pork and Gravy

Salt pork has served and been served by homemakers during slavery, the Great Depression, poverty, and even prosperous times.

* * *

Cut the salt pork into thin slices. Slash the rind in several places. Place in a warmed skillet and fry slowly until browned on both sides, turning often. Remove the salt pork and keep warm. Meanwhile, make "poor man's gravy" by adding enough flour to absorb the fat in the skillet. Slowly stir in milk to make a fairly thick gravy. Pour over the pork and serve.

Alternate "gravy:" After removing the fried pork from the skillet, pour the hot grease from the skillet into a bowl of dark molasses. Stir well and serve along with biscuits and the fried pork.

Note: If the salt pork is excessively salty, place it in cold water, bring to a boil, drain, and then proceed to fry.

Brains and Eggs

Animal brains are another example of soul food/survival food/desirable food. Scientists now caution against eating brains for fear of Creutzfeldt-Jakob disease,[65] but in times past, before so many foods, etc. were "hazardous," people were just thankful for food on the table. Black and white folks of ordinary financial circumstances did not hesitate to consume "brain food," and other innards.

* * *

1 lb. calf's or pig's brains, and water to cover
1 tbsp. vinegar
Dash of salt
Butter or bacon fat
4 eggs

Rinse brains. Place brains in a large pot, cover with water, add vinegar, and a dash of salt. Bring to a boil, cover pot, and simmer for 10 minutes. Drain the brains, and break into pieces. Next heat butter or bacon fat in a skillet, add the brains and heat them. Meanwhile, lightly beat four eggs, and pour them into the skillet. Cook gently until the eggs are set. Serve right away with catsup.

Hog Maw [Stomach] Salad

In the British Isles, particularly Scotland, a popular dish called "haggis" is prepared. It consists of the heart, lungs, and liver of a sheep or calf, etc. mixed with oatmeal and suet, seasoned with salt, pepper and onions, and boiled like a big sausage encased in a "maw" or stomach removed from an animal.[66] The whole dish is eaten, stomach and all.

The Romans, according to history, taught the Scots this idea, but they used a pig's stomach, and filled it with brains, eggs, pineapple (!), etc.[67] "They [black Southerners] make a hog maw salad flavored with celery and green pepper that is so esoteric it is sometimes taken for chicken salad."[68]

* * *

Rinse maws in cold water; place in a pot and cover with water. Bring to a boil. Cover and simmer 4 hours. Remove the fatty parts, chop finely, and cool. Combine with 1 1/2 c. finely-chopped celery, 1 c. finely-chopped onion, and 1/2 c. finely-chopped green pepper. Add mayonnaise to moisten, and season to taste with salt and pepper.

Rice Fritters

Rice is said to have been first brought to Charleston, South Carolina in 1694 by a Dutch brig out of Madagascar.[69] It was successfully cultivated there (and in Louisiana). "Cracked" or low grade rice was frequently part of the slave ration in South Carolina.[70] The slaves incorporated the grains of this grass into their diet, and into dishes which graced the slave-keepers' tables.

From Africa (and Europe) women brought the practice of making fritters. Rice, corn, other vegetables, and fruits came to the dining table in this starchy guise.

* * *

"Rice fritters are made with cold boiled rice. To half a cup add a beaten egg, half a cup of rich milk and enough flour to make a fritter batter. Drop in spoonfuls in a skillet in hot butter and brown on both sides. Serve with honey or with maple syrup or sprinkle with salt and serve as a vegetable."[71]

Corn Fritters

8 large ears of corn, cut three times (not grated)
2 eggs
1 teacup sweet milk (or more, if the corn is not juicy)
2 teaspoonfuls flour
Salt and pepper to taste

Make the mixture the consistency of a soft batter, and fry by spoonfuls in lard or butter.[72]

Fruit Fritters

To prepare the batter:

1 c. flour
1 tsp. sugar
1/2 tsp. salt
2/3 c. milk
2 eggs, well-beaten

Mix the flour, sugar, and salt. Add milk slowly and then gradually add the eggs.[73]

To complete the fruit fritters:

Cut fruit (apple, peach, apricot, pear, banana, or other fruit) in pieces, dip in the fruit fritter batter above and fry in deep hot (375° F.) fat or butter about 3 to 5 minutes or until golden brown. Then remove with skimmer, and place on crumpled soft paper to drain. Sprinkle with powdered sugar and serve with a lemon or other fruit juice sauce.[74]

Jambalaya

A one-pot main course built around rice was characteristic of the black cook's way of stretching the food ration. Start with the starch (a carbohydrate such as rice, potatoes, cornmeal, etc.) and extend it with whatever vegetables, protein, and seasonings might be had. Slaves cooking in their homes for their own families usually had a very limited number of pieces of cookware, so soups, stews, pilaus and other one-pot meals were ideally suited to their situation. Jambalaya shows the influence of black, Spanish, and French food culture.

* * *

2 tbsp. butter
2 onions, chopped

1 tbsp. flour
2 c. water
1 No. 1 (10 1/2-oz.) can tomatoes
1 green pepper, chopped
1 clove garlic, chopped
1 tbsp. parsley, chopped
1 bay leaf
1/4 tsp. thyme
Salt, pepper to taste
1 c. uncooked rice
1 pint cooked shrimp
1 pint oysters

Jambalaya is usually made in an iron pot with a lid —
the Dutch oven type of pot. Into it first is put the butter,
which is allowed to melt. Then the chopped onion, which is
browned; then the flour, which is also browned. Then the
water is added slowly to make a smooth paste. Then add the
tomatoes, green pepper, garlic, parsley, bay leaf, thyme, salt,
pepper, and rice. The lid is put on and the mixture allowed to
simmer for 30 to 45 minutes, until the rice has taken up
nearly all the moisture and is quite done. The mixture should
be stirred occasionally to keep it from sticking. Now add the
shrimp and oysters with liquor. When they have all been
heated through the Jambalaya is ready to serve. (Makes 6
servings.) [75]

Red Rice

Red Rice is usually served as a side-dish, but during
hard times it can be a main course. It is called Creole rice in
Louisiana, Spanish rice in the inland South, Savannah rice in
Georgia, and tomato pilau in Savannah![76]

This dish also resembles *Thiebou dienn*, a post-
European Senegalese dish[77] and *Jolof*, a Gambian rice stew
containing a leafy vegetable and crayfish (rather than pork).[78]

* * *

4 - 6 strips bacon
1 onion, chopped
1 c. uncooked rice

2 c. canned tomatoes, chopped up (including juice)
1/2 c. water
Salt, pepper, and Tabasco sauce to taste

In a large saucepan, fry the bacon until it is crispy. Drain on paper towels. Meanwhile, cook the onion in the bacon fat until it is translucent. Add the rice, and sauté briefly. Stir in the tomatoes, water, and seasonings. Cover tightly and simmer about 20 minutes or until the rice is tender. Crumble the bacon and sprinkle on top of the Red Rice before serving.

Limping Susan

Okra is said to have originated in Africa, and reached this country three centuries ago via the slave trade. It stars in the following Carolina pilau called "Limping Susan," [79] first cousin of the rice and black-eyed pea dish named "Hopping John."

* * *

4 - 6 strips bacon, diced
1 c. okra, sliced
2 c. chicken broth
1 c. uncooked rice
Salt and pepper

In a deep skillet fry the bacon until nearly crisp. Add the okra, and cook until barely tender. Slowly pour in the broth, add the rice, salt and pepper, and bring to a boil. Cover, reduce heat and simmer until the rice is tender, about twenty minutes.

Gumbo

Mary Randolph, in *The Virginia House-wife* (1824) gave American cooks the first printed recipe for cooking okra. She declared the pods to be "very nutritious and easy of digestion." She also presented instructions for making "ochra" soup.

The following recipe for gumbo containing okra appeared in *Housekeeping In Old Virginia*, compiled in 1876. Incidentally, "ki-ngombo" means "okra" in one of the Angolan languages[80], and there are several similar words for okra in other African tongues.

Directions for presenting the dish were also deemed necessary.

* * *

"Cut up two chickens, fry slightly with a little onion, and a few slices pickled pork.

"Put in three or four quarts boiling water, together with pepper and salt, eighteen okras, one-half peck cut up tomatoes.

"Stew one hour and a half." [81]

"It must be dished like soup and eaten with rice; the rice to be boiled dry and served in a vegetable dish; put one or two spoonfuls in a plate and pour the gumbo over it." [82]

Black Pot Catfish Stew

Vegetables comprised a large part of the slave diet. Turnips and turnip greens, cabbage, okra, eggplant, black-eyed peas, sweet potatoes, pumpkins, squash, corn, string beans, beets, etc., were grown by the slaves. In many cases, "Every one is allowed a small piece of good land, which he cultivates as his own." [83]

West African peoples were, for the most part, agriculturists, so naturally when slaves were brought here they incorporated legumes, roots, and grains into their diet to the extent that circumstances permitted.

Since plant foods produced on the property were a great deal cheaper than animal protein foods, the bulk of slave ration was also vegetable.[84]

To season all these nourishing vegetables, black cooks favored pork, which was normally part of their ration. Chicken or fish (as in this recipe) might be added to particular dishes, for slaves were allowed to raise poultry and to fish. (Hook and line, traps, or baskets were used to catch fish and crabs.)[85]

Black Pot Catfish Stew stars the favorite fish of most pre-twentieth-century Southerners, black or white.[86]

* * *

4 medium-size catfish, cleaned and dressed
4 c. water
4 c. Irish potatoes, diced
2 c. onion, chopped
2 c. whole-kernel corn
2 tbsp. butter
2 c. milk
Salt and pepper

Put the fish and the 4 cups of water in a large pot. Bring to a boil, cover and simmer until the fish is flaky. Remove the fish from the liquid, reserving the broth. Remove bones from the fish, and set fish aside.

Add the potatoes and onions to the fish broth, and cook until the vegetables are tender. Add the corn. (If the corn is fresh or frozen, rather than canned, cook it until tender - about 10 minutes.) Stir in the butter, milk, salt and pepper to taste, and the reserved fish. Heat thoroughly and serve.

Alabama Dish

This recipe, dating from slavery days, is very flexible. A more modern version omits the potatoes and adds cream and Parmesan cheese. Slaves were seldom given dairy products for their own use, but, for the master's table, the black cook could create delicacies involving "gifts from the cow."

* * *

2 slices bacon, chopped, or thinly sliced salt pork, diced
1 1/2 c. onion, chopped
8 - 12 new potatoes, preferably unpeeled, small and whole
1 lb. green (string) beans, tips removed, and broken if large
3 medium-sized tomatoes, peeled and chopped

Salt and pepper
1/4 - 1/2 c. water (approximately)

In a large, deep skillet, cook the bacon or salt pork until just crisp; add the onion, and cook until tender. Layer on top the potatoes, string beans, and tomatoes, seasoning each layer with a little salt and pepper. Add a small amount of water to the skillet, cover tightly and simmer over low heat until the vegetables are tender. It may be necessary to add more water.

Potato Salad

Potato salad, featuring the filling and nourishing Irish potato, is often served at church and social meals, and family parties. (In the 1800's, as you probably realize, a homemade dressing was used rather than store-bought mayonnaise.) Local cooks attest that commercial sweet pickle relish is far preferable to chopped-up pickles in potato salad.

* * *

8 medium-size potatoes, unpeeled
2 tbsp. finely-chopped onion
2 tbsp. finely-chopped celery
2 tbsp. sweet pickle relish
2 hard-cooked eggs, chopped
Mayonnaise
1 tsp. dry mustard
Salt and pepper to taste, fresh parsley, paprika

Boil the potatoes in salted water until just tender. Cool and remove skins. Dice. Put the potatoes in a large bowl with the onion, celery, and eggs. Meanwhile, mix together 1/2 c. mayonnaise, the dry mustard, salt, and pepper. Stir this mixture into the potato mixture, adding more mayonnaise as needed to moisten. Cover and chill. Serve garnished with fresh parsley and sprinkled with paprika.

Plantation Shortcake

When the railroad industry needed chefs for their dining cars, they looked to the black race because of their reputation as sterling cooks. Out of sixty-three railroads surveyed in 1921, fifty-one had African-American cooks. Dining car menus listing peanut soup, beef stew, pineapple fritters, biscuits, scalloped oysters, and baked sweet potatoes reflected the decided influence of Southern plantation cooking.[87]

This recipe is an example of Southern black cooking from Southern Pacific's *Our Dining Car Recipes*, a booklet which also includes directions for preparing chicken gumbo, corn fritters, ham smothered in sweet potatoes, pork (pot) pie, and corn custard.

* * *

"Bake a thin layer of corn bread and cut in suitable squares, figuring three squares to one order. Place on one a slice of fried or baked ham, and cover. On the second layer spread slices of breast of chicken and cover with the third. Wash and peel two medium sized fresh mushrooms, slice and saute in butter without browning. Add one-half a teaspoonful and, when well absorbed, one-half cupful of cream. Let boil until thick, or about two minutes, pour over shortcake and serve." [88]

Sweet Potato Biscuits

In the South, during the Civil War, white flour was a luxury. It is said that sweet potatoes were added to biscuit dough so that the flour would go further.[89] Whether a black or white lady first began doing this, who knows? But the resulting sweet potato biscuit recipes are delicious legacies.

* * *

1 lb. sweet potatoes, cooked and peeled
1/2 c. butter
1/2 c. sugar
Dash of salt
2 tbsp. milk
3 1/2 c. all-purpose flour
4 tsp. baking powder
2 tsp. cinnamon

While the sweet potatoes are still hot, add the butter, sugar, salt, and milk. Mix well. In a separate container mix the flour, baking powder, and cinnamon. Stir the dry ingredients into the potato mixture; then knead it gently. Chill the dough 2 - 3 hours. On a lightly floured surface, roll out the dough to a 1/2-inch thickness, and cut out biscuits. Bake on a lightly greased cookie sheet at 400° F. for about 15 minutes or until done.[90]

(Hog) Jowl and Turnip Salad

The steps of preparation in the following heirloom dish are not for the weak-of-stomach:

* * *

"This is an old Virginia dish, and much used in the spring of the year.

"The jowl, which must have been well smoked, must be washed clean, and boiled for three hours. Put in the salad [turnip greens], and boil half an hour; if you boil too long, it will turn yellow. It is also good broiled for breakfast with pepper and butter over it.

"The jaw-bone should be removed before sending to the table; this is easily done by running a knife around the lip and under the tongue. The jowl and salad should always be served with fresh poached eggs." [91]

Dandelion Greens

Malcolm X wrote in his autobiography about hard times in his youth:

"Our mother knew, I guess, dozens of ways to cook things with bread and out of bread. Stewed tomatoes with bread, maybe that would be a meal. Something like French toast, if we had any eggs. Bread pudding, sometimes with raisins in it. If we got hold of some hamburger, it came to the table more bread than meat. . . . But there were times when there wasn't even a nickel and we would be so hungry we were dizzy. My mother would boil a big pot of dandelion greens, and we would eat that." [92]

-27-

Free for the picking, dandelion greens filled many an empty stomach. George Washington Carver, Tuskegee Institute scientist, introduced dandelion greens, chicory, chickweed, pepper grass, and watercress to the college dining hall menu.[93]

* * *

1 qt. dandelion greens
Ham shank
1 tbsp. butter
Salt and pepper to taste
Sliced hard-boiled eggs

"Cut off the coarse roots; wash the leaves thoroughly; steep in salt and water for five hours to remove the bitterness. Boil a ham shank for two hours, throw in the dandelions and cook gently for forty-five minutes; then drain, chop fine; season with butter, pepper and salt. Mince the ham very fine and sprinkle over the greens; spread over sliced hard-boiled eggs and serve hot." [94]

Bread Pudding

"Scald 2 cups stale bread crumbs with 1 quart milk. Cool. Add 1/3 cup sugar, 2 slightly beaten eggs, 1/2 teaspoon salt, 1/4 cup melted butter and 1 teaspoon vanilla. Turn into a buttered baking dish and bake in a slow oven until thick and delicately browned." [95]

Lady Baltimore Cake

"Marse and Missus had good rations for us early on the Fourth [of July]. Then us went to barbecues after the morning chores was done. . . . Old Marse he give us the rations for the barbecues. Every master wanted his [slaves] to be thought well of at the barbecues by the [slaves] from all the other plantations. They had pigs barbecued, and goats; and the missus let the women-folks bake pies, cakes and custards for the barbecue, just 'zactly like it was for the white folks' barbecue . . . . " [96]

Often, when a black slave first made a recipe with which she was unfamiliar, perhaps for an event such as the Fourth of July celebration mentioned above, the mistress (who had not chosen to learn how to cook) read the recipe to the cook (who had not been given the opportunity to learn to read).[97] After preparing a new recipe a few times, the cook more or less memorized it, but often modified or embellished it according to her own taste. One mammy is quoted as telling her owner's daughters, "Nobody but [blacks] go in thar [the kitchen]. Sit in de parlor wed 'er book in y'or hand like little white ladies." [98]

Recipes similar to "Lady Baltimore Cake" (and the "Molasses Cake" on the next page) have been popular in the black community for decades. When a preparer took such a cake to a group event, she wanted it to be a "name cake;" that is to say, a cake which she would be happy to claim ownership of, proud to have her name said when people asked who baked the item.[99]

* * *

"1 cupful of butter, 2 cupfuls of granulated sugar, 1 cupful of milk, 3 1/2 cupfuls of flour, 3 level teaspoonfuls of baking powder, the whites of 6 eggs. Cream the butter and sugar gradually. Sift together the flour and baking powder 3 times. Add the milk, and lastly the eggs; for flavoring use 1 teaspoonful each of lemon and vanilla. One-half of this recipe makes a fair sized cake. For icing use the following:

"*Icing for Lady Baltimore Cake*: 3 cupfuls of granulated sugar, 1 cupful of boiling water, whites of 3 eggs, 1 cupful of chopped raisins, 1 cupful of chopped nut meats, 5 figs, cut or ground. Stir together the sugar and water, let boil until it spins a thread, pour over the stiffly beaten whites of the egg, beat well, adding the fruit gradually.

"Bake the cake in layers, putting together with the icing." [100]

Molasses Cake

"At breakfast the field hands ate fried meat, corn bread and molasses. When they went to the house for

dinner they were given some kind of vegetable along with pot liquor and milk. When the day's work was done and it was time for the evening meal there was the fried meat again with the molasses and the corn bread. They ate this kind of food every day in the week. The only variation was on Sunday when they were given the seconds of the flour and a little molasses so that they might make a cake. No other sweetening was used except molasses. " [101]

* * *

2 c. all-purpose flour
1 tsp. baking powder
1 tsp. ginger
2 eggs
1/2 c. soft shortening
1/4 c. milk (approximately)
1 c. molasses

Mix the first three ingredients. In a separate bowl beat together the remaining ingredients. Combine the two mixtures, stirring well. (Add a little more milk if needed to make a thick, but pourable batter.) Pour into a greased 9x13-inch pan, and bake at 375° F. for about 50 minutes or until done.

Benne Seed Wafers or Cookies

In 1808 Thomas Jefferson sent Anne Cary Randolph "some seed of the Beny." He explained, "It was brought to S. Carolina from Africa by the negroes, who alone have hitherto cultivated it in the Carolinas and Georgia. They bake it in their bread, boil it with greens, enrich their broth & c." [102]

Nowadays sesame seeds can be found on hamburger buns, in candies and cookies — most especially sesame crackers and the traditional sesame cookies (wafers) baked in South Carolina. (For trivia lovers: In Myrtle Beach, South Carolina, sesame seed cookies are known as "good luck cookies." [103])

* * *

1/2 c. butter, at room temperature
1 c. firmly packed light brown sugar
1 egg
1 tsp. vanilla extract
1 c. all-purpose flour
3/4 c. toasted sesame (benne) seeds
1/4 tsp. salt

Beat together the butter and sugar until light and fluffy. Add the egg and vanilla and beat to combine. Stir in the remaining ingredients. Pipe the cookie dough (or drop, using a 1/2-teaspoon measuring spoon) onto cookie sheets which have been lined with aluminum foil. Place the little bits of dough two inches apart (they spread out as they bake). Bake at 325° F. for 10 to 15 minutes or until the cookies are a light golden brown. Cool on a rack until the cookies "release" from the foil. Store in airtight containers.

Note: To toast sesame seeds, spread them on a baking pan, and toast at 275° F. for about 10 minutes.

Molasses Taffy

"If we had 'freshments [at a frolic] it would alwas' be ginger cakes, parched peanuts an lasses candy. Now we had regular candy pullings too and dey wuz a heap o' fun," [104]

reminisced Mississippian Robert Weatherby.

"We would have candy pulls from cooked molasses...." [105]

* * *

2 c. molasses
1 c. sugar
2 tsp. butter
1 tbsp. apple cider vinegar
2 tbsp. lemon juice
A few grains salt
1/4 tsp. baking soda

In a large pot boil the molasses and sugar until a small portion of it forms a soft ball when dropped in icy cold water.

Add the butter, vinegar, lemon juice, and salt. Boil again until a little bit will harden when dropped in the cold water. Remove from the heat and quickly stir in the soda. Mix well, and pour the candy on a greased pan, platter, or marble slab. When the taffy is cool enough to handle, cut into sections, grease your hands and start pulling the candy out in a rope, then folding it back together. (This incorporates air into the taffy.) When the candy is light in color and stiff, cut it into bite size pieces (scissors work nicely for this) or twist it into the lengths you desire. Wrap each piece in wax paper.[106]

And speaking of candy and times of its abundance:

"Christmas was de time o' all times on dat old plantation. Dey don't have no such as dat now. Every child brought a stockin' up to de Big House to be filled. Dey all wanted one o' de mistis' stockin's, 'cause now she weighted nigh on to three hundred pounds. Candy and presents was put in piles for everyone." [107]

". . . [O]n Christmas Day . . . Marse Lordnorth and Marse Alec give us everything you could name to eat: cake of all kinds, fresh meat, lightbread, turkeys, chickens, ducks, geese and all sorts of wild game. There was always plenty of pecans, apples and dried peaches too at Christmas." [108]

"They give us cake at Christmas and eggnog and 'silly-bug' [syllabub?]. Eggnog is made from whites of eggs and 'silly-bug' from yallers. You have to churn the whiskey and yallers to make 'silly-bug.'" [109]

Conclusion

Two hundred years ago a new arrival from Africa, boiling greens over the hearth fire, probably could not envision her individual role in establishing Southern/Survival/Soul foodways. But, collectively, with her black sisters (and brothers), she helped to create America's most comforting cuisine.

Notes

Narrative Source #1 (NS1): Ronald Killion and Charles Walker, ed., *Slavery Time When I Was Chillun Down on Marster's Plantation: Interviews with Georgia Slaves*, The Beehive Press, Savannah, GA, 1973.

Narrative Source #2 (NS2): Norman R. Yetman, *Life Under the "Peculiar Institution"*, Holt, Rinehart, and Winston, Inc., New York, 1970.

Narrative Source #3 (NS3): Charles L. Perdue, Jr., Thomas E. Barden, and Robert K. Phillips, ed., *Weevils in the Wheat: Interviews with Virginia Ex-Slaves*, University Press of Virginia, Charlottesville, VA, 1976.

Narrative Source #4 (NS4): George P. Rawick, ed., *The American Slave: A Composite Autobiography*, Greenwood Press, Westport, CT, 1972.

(If a specific date is not listed for a narrative excerpt, it is from the late 1930's, the time of the Federal Writers Project.)

[1] Louis P. DeGouy, *The Gold Cook Book*, Greenberg Publishing, New York, 1947, p. vii.

[2] John Egerton, *Southern Food*, University of North Carolina Press, Chapel Hill, NC, 1987, p. 15.

[3] Henry Steele Commager, ed., *The Illustrated History of the Civil War*, Exeter Books, New York, 1976, p. 12.

[4] NS1, p. 138, interview with Melvin Smith, July 15, 1937.

[5] *Ibid.*, p. 26, interview with James Bolton, Athens, GA, 1937.

[6] *Ibid.*, p. 62, interview with Callie Elder, Athens, GA.

[7] NS2, p. 331, interview with Willis Winn, age 115, near Marshall, TX.

[8] Ruth Coder Fitzgerald, *A Different Story: A Black History of Fredericksburg, Stafford and Spotsylvania, Virginia*, Unicorn, 1979, pp. 19, 20, quoting Carter G. Woodson, *The Education of the Negro Prior to 1861*, New York, 1915, p. 9.

[9] Diane Dipiero, "Together At Christmas," *Colonial Homes*, Dec. 1994, p. 28.

[10] NS1, p. 25, interview with James Bolton, Athens, GA, 1937.

[11] *Ibid.*, p. 142, interview with John Cole, Athens, GA.

[12] *Ibid.*, p. 25, interview with James Bolton, Athens, GA, 1937.

[13] Walter Terry, *The Dance In America*, Revised Ed., Harper & Row Publishers, New York, 1971, p. 157.

[14] NS1, p. 143, interview with Estella Jones, Augusta, GA.

[15] NS3, p. 294, interview with Annie Wallace, Culpeper, VA, April 2, 1940.

[16] *Ibid.*, pp. 49-50, interview with Mrs. Fannie Berry, Petersburg, VA, February 26, 1937.

[17] *Ibid.*, interview with Bailey Cunningham, Starkey, VA, early 1938.

[18] Dipiero.

[19] NS1, p. 62, interview with Estella Jones, Augusta, GA.

[20] NS2, p. 332, interview with Willis Winn, age 115, near Marshall, TX.

[21] *Ibid.*, p. 124, interview with John Finnely, age 86, Fort Worth, TX.

[22] NS1, p. 25, interview with James Bolton, Athens, GA, 1937.

[23] *Ibid.*, p. xvii.

[24] NS3, pp. 49-50, interview with Cornelius Garner, Norfolk, VA.

[25] *Ibid.*, pp. 320, 322, interview with Nancy Williams, Norfolk, VA, May 18, 1937.

[26] NS1, p. 24, interview with James Bolton, Athens, GA, 1937.

[27] NS2, p. 12, interview with Lucretia Alexander, age 89, Little Rock, AR.

[28] NS1, p. 82, interview with Charlie Hudson, Athens, GA, 1938.

[29] NS2, p. 335, interview with Clara C. Young, approximate age 95, Monroe County, MS.

[30] NS3, p. 93, commenting on NS1, Vol. 1.

[31] NS1, p. 45, interview with Willis Cofer, Athens, GA, March 1938.

[32] Fitzgerald, p. 10.

[33] NS1, p. 21, interview with James Bolton, Athens, GA, 1937.

[34] Francis Coleman Rosenberger, *Virginia Reader: A Treasury of Writings*, E. P. Dutton & Company, 1948, New York, pp. 491-492, from Booker T. Washington, *The Story of My Life and Work*, J. L. Nichols & Co., Atlanta, GA, 1900.

[35] NS1, p. 62, interview with Callie Elder, Athens, GA.

[36] Paul D. Escott, *Slavery Remembered*, The University of North Carolina Press, Chapel Hill, NC, 1979, p. 39.

[37] B. A. Botkin, ed., *Lay My Burden Down: A Folk History of Slavery*, University of Chicago Press, Chicago, IL, 1945, p. 60, 121, quoting Mary Reynolds, Louisiana.

[38] NS1, p. 137, interview with George Washington Browning, Walton County, GA, January 25, 1937.

[39] Thomas D. Cockrell and Michael B. Ballard, ed., *A Mississippi Rebel in the Army of Northern Virginia: The Civil War Memoirs of Private David Holt*, Louisiana State University Press, Baton Rouge, LA, 1995, pp. 37-38.

[40] NS1, p. 93, interview with Robert Shepherd, Athens, GA, 1938.

[41] Rosenberger, p. 491, from Washington.

[42] NS1, p. 15, interview with Jasper Battle, Athens, GA, July 1938.

[43] *Ibid.*, p. 56, interview with Benny Dillard, Athens, GA, 1938.

[44] *Ibid.*, p. 77, interview with Charlie Hudson, Athens, GA, 1938.

[45] John Hebron Moore, *The Emergence of The Cotton Kingdom in the Old Southwest, Mississippi, 1770-1860*, Louisiana State University Press, Baton Rouge, LA, 1988, p. 91, quoting from NS4, Vol. VII, Pt. 2, pp. 525, 534, 537, 602-603, and Vol. VIII, Pt. 3, pp. 1185-1186.

[46] NS1, p. 105, interview with Neal Upson, Athens, GA.

[47] Patricia C. McKissack and Frederick L. McKissack, *Christmas in the Big House, Christmas in the Quarters*, Scholastic Inc., New York, 1994, p. 64.

[48] NS1, p. 56, interview with Benny Dillard, Athens, GA, 1938.

[49] NS2, p. 58, interview with Peter Clifton, age 89, Winnsboro, SC.

[50] NS1, p. 126, interview with Rhodus Walton, Lumpkin, GA.

[51] *Ibid.*, p. 56, interview with Benny Dillard, Athens, GA, 1938.

[52] Jessica B. Harris, *The Welcome Table*, Simon and Schuster, Inc., New York, 1995, pp. 21-22.

[53] NS1, pp. 126-127, interview with Susan Castle, Athens, GA.

[54] NS3, p. 294, interview with "Aunt" Susan Kelly, Guinea, Gloucester County, VA, April 14, 1937.

[55] Eugene D. Genovese, *Roll, Jordan, Roll: The World the Slaves Made*, Pantheon Books, New York, 1974, p. 547, quoting NS4, Vol. VI, Part 2, p. 54.

[56] Genovese, p. 548, quoting Work Projects Administration, Workers of the Writers Program, State of Virginia, *Negro in Virginia*, New York, 1940, p. 70.

[57] NS1, p. 105, interview with Neal Upson, Athens, GA.

[58] NS2, p. 331, interview with Willis Winn, age 115, Marshall, TX.

[59] *Ibid.*, p. 67, interview with Cheney Cross, age 90+, near Evergreen, AL.

[60] John Hebron Moore, p. 92, quoting NS4, Vol. VII, Pt. 2, pp. 369, 626-627, 654-655.

[61] NS2, p. 281, interview with Gus Smith, age 92, Rolla, MO.

[62] Joe Gray Taylor, *Eating, Drinking, and Visiting in the South*, Louisiana State University Press, Baton Rouge, LA, 1982, p. 85.

[63] Evan Jones, *American Food: The Gastronomic Story*, Second Edition, Random House, New York, 1981, p. 106.

[64] Marion W. Flexner, *Dixie Dishes*, Hale, Cushman & Flint, Boston, 1941, p. 64.

[65] "Doctors: Think twice about eating squirrel brains," Associated Press, Frankfort, KY, September 8, 1997.

[66] Evelyn Abraham Benson, ed., *Penn Family Recipes: Cooking Recipes of Wm. Penn's Wife, Gulielma*, George Shumway, Publisher, York, PA, 1966, p. 8.

[67] André L. Simon, *A Concise Encyclopaedia of Gastronomy*, Bramhall House, New York, 1952, p. 434-435.

[68] Jones, p. 101.

[69] Editors of American Heritage, *The American Heritage Cookbook and Illustrated History of American Eating and Drinking*, Simon and Schuster, Inc., New York, 1964, p. 535.

[70] David Doar, "Rice and Rice Planting in the South Carolina Low Country," *The Charleston Museum Contributions*, No. 8, Charleston, SC, Charleston Museum, 1936, p. 32.

[71] 1918 newspaper clipping, author's private collection.

[72] Marion Cabell Tyree, *Housekeeping in Old Virginia*, John P. Morton and Co., Louisville, KY, 1879, p. 243.

[73] Lillie S. Lustig, S. Claire Sondheim, Sarah Rensel, *The Southern Cook Book of Fine Old Recipes,* Culinary Arts Press, Reading, PA, 1939, p. 28.

[74] *Ibid.*

[75] Flexner, p. 35.

[76] Egerton, p. 309.

[77] Candy Sagon, "Red Rice, Fritters and a Taste Called 'Home,'" *Washington Post*, February 8, 1995, pp. E1, E11.

[78] Edna Lewis with Mary Goodbody, *In Pursuit of Flavor*, Alfred A. Knopf, New York, 1988, p. 57.

[79] Egerton, p. 304.

[80] Jessica B. Harris, *Iron Pots and Wooden Spoons*, Atheneum, NY, 1989, p. 74.

[81] Tyree, p. 213, recipe attributed to Mrs. David S. Reid, Roanoke County, VA.

[82] *Ibid.*

[83] Stacy Gibbons Moore, "Established and Well Cultivated: Afro-American Foodways in Early Virginia," *Virginia Cavalcade*, Virginia State Library and Archives, Richmond, VA, Autumn 1989, pp. 74-75.

[84] Taylor, p. 87.

[85] *Ibid.*, p. 86.

[86] *Ibid.*

[87] Harris, *The Welcome Table*, p. 31.

[88] *Our Dining Car Recipes*, Southern Pacific, p. 7, courtesy of Western Railway Museum, Berkeley, CA.

[89] *Southern Living*, Vol. 12, No. II, Nov. 1977, The Progressive Farmer Co., Birmingham, AL, p. 214.

[90] Recipe courtesy Ronald G. Gimbert, Goldsboro, NC.

[91] Tyree, p. 130, recipe attributed to Mrs. Philip Withers, Lynchburg, VA.

[92] Malcolm X with the assistance of Alex Haley, *The Autobiography of Malcolm X*, Ballantine Books, New York, 1965, p. 13.

[93] James Trager, *Foodbook*, Grossman Publishers, New York, 1970, p. 253.

[94] *The Picayune's Creole Cookbook*, Second Edition, The Picayune, New Orleans, LA, 1901, reprinted by Dover Publications, Inc., New York, 1971, p. 223.

[95] Old newspaper clipping, author's private collection.

[96] Botkin, pp. 143-144.

[97] Payne Bournight Tyler, *The Virginia Presidential Homes Cookbook*, Williamsburg Publishing Co., Williamsburg, VA, 1987, p. 3.

[98] Annie Laurie Broidrick of Mississippi quoting "old 'mammy Harriet,'" Broidrick, manuscript *Recollection of Thirty Years Ago*, State Department of Archives and History, Louisiana State University, Baton Rouge, LA, pp. 6-7, in Genovese, p. 354.

[99] Ruth L. Gaskins, *A Good Heart and A Light Hand*, Simon and Schuster, New York, 1968, p. 68.

[100] Mary Eleanor Kramer, "New Year's Cakes and Drinks," *The Farmer's Wife*, January 1914, author's private collection.

[101] NS1, p. 118, interview with George Womble, Athens, GA, 1937.

[102] Stacy Gibbons Moore, p. 83.

[103] Jones, p. 105.

[104] John Hebron Moore, p. 92, quoting NS4, Vol. VIII, Part 3, p. 1245, and Vol. X, Part 5, pp. 2241-2242.

[105] NS2, p. 167, interview with Marriah Hines.

[106] Adapted from recipe in Flexner, p. 150.

[107] NS2, p. 190, interview with Prince Johnson, Clarksdale, MS.

[108] NS1, p. 138, interview with Georgia Baker, approximate age 85, Athens, GA.

[109] NS2, p. 331, interview with Willis Winn, age 115, near Marshall, TX.